A Crow's Breakfast

Poems

from

The Low Road

R.J. Looney

Some of these poems have appeared in various forms in *Thunder Sandwich, The Dead Mule School of Southern Literature, Fried Chicken and Coffee, Salt Journal, Open Writing, Kleft Jaw, Pigeonbike: Beyond the Broken Bridge, The Local Voice, The Opinion,* and *The Outlaw Poetry Network.*

Thanks to: Carter Monroe, Jim Chandler, and Terri Adair-Looney for their advice and encouragement; The White Water Tavern, Maxine's, and Mid-Town Billiards for a place to hide and the inspiration to write; and to all my dear friends for their support.

Inside art by Susan Wimberly

Back Cover photo by Terri-Adair Looney, White Water Tavern, Little Rock, AR

Contact: randaljlooney@live.com

Published by
Rank Stranger Press

Southern poetry can be a conceited art form. It's like we think somehow we have a monopoly in terms of "characters." The fact is that every living human is a "character." The task of some poets is to record via the narrative and understand that reality contains its own natural symbolism. Many do this on varying levels. Yet, there are always cracks in the construction of reality even when the subject of exploration seems cut and dried. The genius of RJ Looney comes in his melding of the perception of said cracks with the not always obvious narrative. He has the unique ability to look "at" something while looking beyond it at the same time. He understands that life always boils down to perception and perspective and that the "right" answer isn't always unique. — *Carter Monroe*

I won't hesitate to say that RJ Looney's *A Crow's Breakfast* is the best first collection I've ever read. Looney is bound to rattle some cages in the poetry world. It's an astounding set of narrative poems that resonates in an old Southern soul like mine. — *Jim Chandler*

This book of poems is dedicated to the ideas, people, places, and things that are responsible for its existence.

CONTENTS

It Is Poetry

What makes me do this?
I wake up at 2:30 am every Monday
most times with the annoying chorus
to a *Foghat* or *Juice Newton* song
from my misspent youth
looping on the worn grooves
in the semi-permanent acetate of my brain
pictures of the past 50 years begin to surface
I will not find sleep again for at least 2 hours
if at all this morning
re-living those images

Those people
Those places
Those events
asking questions, telling tales such as

"Why did all those bad things happen?"
"How did heroin take him away?"
"How could someone turn their back on their own child?"
"Wish I could talk to my grandparents."
"My family is driving me bat shit crazy!"
"Will my grandchildren be safe in this world?"
"My job is driving me bat shit crazy."

"I wish I could put back the can of peanuts I stole through the taped up hole in the hundred year old window of that store in Independence County. Wish I could take back the rock I threw into another window at 15 and the gas I stole a few years later that landed me in the Craighead County hoosegow."

"Racing Scotty Williams and him passing me in his '74 Chevy ¾ ton with a 454, I in my '71 Chevy C-10, 350 4-barrel Quadrajet spewing 65 cent per gallon dead dinosaurs into its belly. We were on top of the White River bridge on Arkansas 122 in 1981 traveling at 120+mph.

Both pickups filled with a good portion of the male segment of our high school student body. Could have easily crashed and burned like my brother in-law did a few years later. Why him and not us?"

"The taste of bubble gum lip gloss in 8th grade, her tanned body and brown eyes, and something that does not count as personal growth occurring in my pants… with a REAL girl present. 1977. Jesus Christ!"

"Why did I pick THAT for a major in college?"
"Why do I drink so much?"
"Did I take the trash cans to the street yesterday afternoon? I know I thought about it."
"Shit! I don't have any cash money to feed the parking meter."

Later in the day at lunch
my mind goes back
to what I thought about earlier that morning

"I need to write a poem about racing Scotty. I've written poems about a lot of all it already. Won't ever forget it."

Then I realize what it is
that makes me wake up at 2:30 in the morning
thinking about all that wonderful, hateful, depressing, boring, joyous,
and sometimes embarrassing stuff that has happened in my life

It is poetry
I create it to survive

Sacrifice

The Earth
gave off a cool breath
as the sun touched the hills
The Weatherman called it
"radiational cooling"
I looked up from my world
barricaded in the sandbox
with dump trucks and dozers
and watched you open the gate
on the east side of the house
the act of raising the rope latch
was a poem
penned in the ink of grace
on the velum of patience
My eyes followed
as you crossed the yard
toward the chicken coup
You reached inside
snatched up an older pullet
destined for dumplings
She'd never be a hen
those strong hands
only minutes before graceful
now gripped the bird
in sacrificial restraint
and committed a murder
tender years couldn't understand
blood on the feathers
made me want to swallow all the colors
I had ever seen, heard, tasted or touched
and hide them in my belly
after supper you read to me
the story of Abraham and Isaac

Catalpa

Cool water dipped from the well
tasted metallic
sun rising over the pin oaks
laundry starting to boil
soap couldn't get it as clean
catfish for supper...maybe

We thought about eating the beans
from your limbs that summer
after the garden dried up
and her milk did too
then baby Russell went on
what did we have to lose?
maybe a window would open
after that door closed in our faces

I always heard the beans
were certain death
we didn't chance it

Your plump black and green worms
with the neon juice-guts
will entice the biggest catfish
to eat my hook
falling off your big green leaves
their temporary quarters
is a Luzianne chicory coffee can
moist dirt and leaves on top
blocks the August sun
on the walk to the river

Open-face Mitchell spinning reel
cast into boiling, swirling waters
can't tell a bite from the current

and then

Hook set in your grisly jaw
we're both hungry
an honorable struggle
old Darwin was right
the strong survive

Hush puppies
sweet onion
consumed
underneath your shade
praise Jesus

Delta Town

Late-night and you're asleep now
but you were awake in the sun
shouting, crying, and flashing your news
spilling your blood, it flows southward
toward the outlet of your wicked bowels
where you digest the minions of your arrant culture
cutting through the softness of your billowy heart
the machine moves coolly through filthy water
splashing up to freeze on winter sidewalks
passing your gray and brown buildings
dotted and speckled with brilliant colors
displaying your toolkit
used for sensory and physical control
your veins are branching main streets
one for us and one for them
your skin is a matrix of depression
freckled with laconic religious fervor
a vehicle for counterfeit wit
a tunnel of poorly concealed hypocrisy
mingling too close to alcoholic abandon
and lower class cavorting
juvenile in action yet wise in direction
irony in the proudness of your bigoted bonds
your image fades in my rear-view mirror
as I travel on to the next one
your twin in nature
yet different in name

'64 Suicide Lincoln

Daddy came home from work
one Wednesday in July at 2 pm
smelling like beer
not talking to anybody
after that he didn't stray too far away
spending most of what would be his last year
in mam-maw's old tractor shed
playing a peavey Strat copy
through a beat up matching amp
he'd picked up at Pancho's Pawn & Loan

We could tell when he was on the Yellowstone
amp cranked up to 11
the neighbors up the hill
would raise hell at us on the party-line
to make him stop

August was hot as a malaria fever
and he wrote a whole catalog
of songs that didn't rhyme
with mean-sounding titles like

Burn Up World

'64 Suicide Lincoln and

Murderous Bible

When October rolled around
he took Uncle Junior's car trailer
to the junkyard and returned with ten car fenders
mostly GM products

November afternoons
were spent with Old Milwaukee

and the little savage bolt-action .22
shooting them full of holes
or pinging in thumb-sized dents
with a 2 lb. ball peen hammer
other times working them over
with pitted leather work boots or gloved fists

In the gray of winter
he took the fenders
and set to practicing
the trade he'd learned
at 17 in reformatory
skills acquired as payment
for a well placed
and equally deserved shovel
delivered to the face of his own daddy
to sober him up
the patched metal fenders
once again smooth as glass
primed and begging to shine
with paint he couldn't afford

St. Patrick's Day
called to the neighbors up the hill
to light out for New Orleans
so Daddy liberated some 20 odd gallons
of John Deere green from their shop
and sprayed his fenders with it
suspended from the tractor shed rafters
like ornaments on a brown Christmas tree

I came home from a party
Sunday morning after he'd finished them
still drunk on malt wine
and saw the light from the shed
a cold north wind

banged the open double doors around
those old fenders bumped each other
like bleached out cow bones
making hollow thumping sounds
scratching away their new coating of stolen love
he was slumped down in a chair facing them
one spent .22 shell on the concrete floor
a blue dot between his eyes
flowing crimson into open coveralls

We never took the fenders down
and on days when I know
the wind is just right
I'll drive out there
open up the doors and play
Daddy's two chord angry songs
through that fuzzy old amp
behind the hollow boney beat
of his memory

Hidden

We lost that old house
40 years ago in a fire
ol' Fagan started it on the back porch
knocked a coal oil lamp off the handrail
not an arsonist; he was scared
a cat ran under his legs
that old cypress went up like newsprint
Fagan lit out and never came back

Aunt Linda gave birth to uncle brace
but we all thought they were siblings
even after Aunt Linda got married
to a geologist eight years later
Geemom took that story to her grave

An old hackberry took over
after the house left
one of the kids hid a prince albert can
in the crotch of the trunk
some 80 odd years ago
placed inside were two clay marbles
a screech owl feather
a tin solider of WWI vintage
and a secret note
from a school house sweetheart

The tree still stands
growing around that metal pocket
slowly rusting away the truth

$30 Hat

She was born Mary in Hogeye, Arkansas
some say 1920
they all called her grit
she walked on hard ground barefoot
until she got her first pair of shoes at 10
her pa was meaner than her ma
and that was pretty damn mean

...so grit left her place behind
with the Wallace's up the road
lit out for California at 12

In Marysville 1932
she picked peaches
til her knuckles turned blue
but she thought there could be
something else that she might do
to make a dollar a day

Lordy, grit found out awful quick
how backseat encounters never stick
they just leave you wantin' more
and make you meaner

Come here sister
now look at that
grit's got a man
with a 30 dollar hat
she's gonna show him
where it's at
Lord that man
wears a 30 dollar hat

Well grit was tough

and she was hard
sometimes she'd sleep
out in the yard
when the skeeters didn't bite
and ticks didn't stick
the dogs growled low
and the air hung thick
she'd dream
that she was all that
sportin' a man
with a 30 dollar hat

For a minute she was
when she was 20
a banker in town
took a fancy to her dark eyes
and tender body
he paid her rent and food
until she come up pregnant
his wife found out
and divorced him
paid for Grit's baby boy
and then adopted him

She moved out to the desert
where whorin' was almost legal
and it was
by the time she saved enough to quit

Now grit is fiddlin'
with a color TV
in Nevada, Las Vegas
1973
rabbit ears
vodka tonic
hell it all comes in
clearer now

she'd sit there every night
watching "M*A*S*H"
and "Love American Style"
sometimes the old hard life
would come back on her
she'd pour more liquor on it and grin

Knowing nobody can't touch her
and nobody owns
any small piece of her ass
no matter how much
they paid for their hat

100 Degrees

Sun ain't even up
it's already 80 degrees
plantin' these flowers
prunin' these trees
all them people in that office
workin' in the cool
shoulda done like my brother
and stayed in school
might have made more
than a handyman
that's what my first wife said

We got married in '74
she always wanted more, more, more
took the two kids and left me here
never did like me drinkin' beer
ain't seen nor heard from them
guess it's almost 30 years
said she wanted to raise the kids up right
guess that's why I didn't put up much of a fight
she couldn't cook worth a damn anyhow

Now I'm glad I got Linda
to keep house and the books
she don't raise too much hell
or give me them looks
when I come home drunk
and she don't know where I've been
just says she was "worried"
and goes back to readin' again

Paintin' these old houses
fixin' their doors
put in a new sink
or a laminate floor

gettin' too old to do this shit anymore
I need to move to the mountains
and breathe in that air
could probably quit drinkin'
if I moved up there
aw, who am I foolin'?....it's almost 1
wonder what people that don't drink do for fun?
guess I'll never know

Yeah, it's houses
not pictures I paint
but I never claimed
to be something I ain't
the sun on this roof
is burnin' my knees
hope I can get to Rudy's by 3
if I get there early
I can get the best table
as much money as I spend in there
you'd think they'd be able
to save it for me, but they won't

Guess I'll pick up my tools
rake up the last of these leaves
I'm just about through
and it's 100 degrees

The Dove

Astrid hid in the potting shed
waiting for Oscar to return
from the masonic lodge
he'd violated her trust
and her womanhood
something she couldn't get back
she poured over seed catalogs
all that winter
while the wood stove burned
and the kettle steamed
and the cat cuddled and purred
against her feet
this time she would not miss her mark
the clop of the horse's hooves
coming up the drive
the snowflakes getting bigger
they tell her she's alive
the brake on the buggy
outside the door
the shovel comes down
Oscar is no more

The Flood

We bought that car in '86
a Cougar, electric blue
half paid with the tax return
the year before we had you
it never blew a gasket
always met our needs
mostly traveled around the countryside
at gravel road speed

I remember plain as day
when the damn thing quit
on the low water bridge
and the creek washed us away

I could barely see out the window
the one that you went through
the car filled up with water
 it was all that I could do
to grab your little body
and hold on to you tight
guess I finally had to let go
'cause there was nothing else I could do
desperation as a last resort
still don't make it right

I looked to Jesus for a time
to help me in my search
to lend a little comfort
but now I won't go back to church
"the Lord moves in mysterious ways"
what the hell is that all about?
if that's true why didn't he reach out his arms
and lift you safely out?

Now my Momma's Bible

sits rotting on the shelf
I'd never believe in heaven again
if god assured me himself

Your little sister...she's still with us
off to college in the fall
we've kept her close
too close maybe
sheltered from the world and all
we couldn't stand to lose another
as beautiful as you

All these years
she never asked us
and we never volunteered
to tell her why
on a sunny day
we'd be smiling
but our eyes were filled with tears

The Path

I've seen you take this path
at least a thousand days before

I wonder if it's just a job
or maybe something more
that keeps you in your dreadful space
up on the 7th floor

Your suit immaculate
pressed and neat
yet confidence lacking
in your stride
keeps your breathing
still in time

"Did I leave the iron on?"

What are the sounds and smells
inside your house?

These things I ponder
at my window
thirty feet
above our wintry street

January '51

White smoke boiled from the tailpipe
like a July thunderhead
1948 Plymouth Special Deluxe
parted an icy puddle
placed by god
in red clay and gravel
yellow stained fingers
steadied the wheel

Hill people looked out
between the muntins
of the front door window
cold metal knob smoothed
from decades of turning
the young girl lay
sweating in a bloody bed
birthing a daughter destined
to her mother's fate

"Oh Lordy…"
to nobody in particular

Maybe a prayer for strength
do this thing one more time
not so much different
from birthing calves with Daddy
sometimes they made it, sometimes not

"It's gonna be okay, Marlene"

17 hours later

Wrapped and screaming child
placed on the bib overalls of her father
waiting by the wood stove

"Can I see her now?"

A clean white sheet covered the mess
and the face of an angel

Miss Ass Cheeks in A Halter Top

Alonzo drove a 1951 Pontiac Chieftain Tutone
turquoise over cream
always parked in the side-yard
between our house and Ms. Blevins'
never under the shade of the pecan
where the dashboard would be safe from the sun
but the sap played hell with the paint job

He was my momma's little brother
though I never called him uncle
and he never went to work
like other grown folks
yet he always had money
the government took care of him
after he'd come back from what momma called "Overseas"
Alonzo called it "In Country"
he said the pictures were still in his head
he tried to make them go away
by pouring liquor on them
or smoking them out of his brain
with sticky hash he kept in 35 mm film containers
it would "drift 'em out to the edges" he'd say
but they always came back
most times more real than before it seemed
he never told any of us about what they looked like
but by the way they upset him we didn't much want to know
he spent most of his days and nights on the back porch
slept out there year round on an old rusty iron bed-stead
sometimes people would come over to see him
dropping off or picking up 35 mm film containers
when they'd leave he'd head to the county line in that chieftain
bottles clinking in a sack when he stomped back up on the porch

He was really the closest thing to a daddy I ever had
we shared a love for baseball

St. Louis Cardinals in particular
one of my favorite Christmas presents was from him
a red plastic bat and ball set when I was about 4
for several summers many afternoons were spent in the side-yard
working on my batting stance
Alonzo pitching south paw
holding a beer in his right hand

His car was like a magic carpet to me
sometimes he would drive me out to the ball diamond
on muggy summer nights
we'd open the triangle side windows on the way
letting the damp river bottom air in to slap our faces
closing them when the mosquitoes got too bad
he'd laugh and tell me
he didn't want my blood
on his tuck and roll upholstery

"If they's gonna be any bodily fluids spilled it's gonna be *MINE* and
HER'S on the *BACK* seat!"

Then he'd punch me in the arm
the Chieftain rolling up under the vapor lights
Alonzo holding a lit Winston between the fingers of his left hand
shaking them in her direction
the crowd in the bleachers seemed to cheer her on
hell even the players on the field would watch her walk by
Alonzo cooing "Miss Ass Cheeks in a halter top"
under his breath and take a drag on the cigarette

When that big Pontiac finally blew a head gasket
I was 14 years old
it set up in the side-yard
further back from the clothesline
tires rotting and paint collecting rust
the neighbor kid across the pasture
shot the windows and lights out within a couple months

Alonzo bought a rusted out Roadrunner
somebody had tried to cover up the rust with gray primer
it looked like blood leaking through a Band-Aid
I felt sorry for both those cars
the same way you feel sorry for a kid
that doesn't have a coat in winter

I was home from school on a snow day a couple years later
me and Alonzo were the only people in the house
I was watching re-runs of *The Big Valley* in the front room
he was on the back porch asleep
a long black car pulled up in the driveway
two men got out and walked to the back porch
I heard the door on the back porch slam
Alonzo hollered "I'm goin' up the road for a few minutes"
leaving with the men in the black car
that was the last thing I heard him say
fact is, nobody ever heard from him again
or found out what happened to him
he must have had the keys to both cars
with him that day because we never found them
when we went through his stuff
momma had Mr. Tompkins up the road
put a new ignition switch in that roadrunner
I started driving it and worked on it after school and weekends
learned a lot from it and it eventually became a good car

Momma passed away not long after I graduated high school
I was going to vo-tech to be a diesel mechanic
still driving that Roadrunner
sometimes people would drive by on the road
stop in and ask to buy Alonzo's old rotted and rusty Pontiac
finally I agreed to sell it
telling the guy to come back the next Saturday afternoon

Late Saturday morning I went out to the car

the biggest chicken snake I ever saw
crawled out from under it and slithered off into the pasture
I opened the driver's side door and sat down on the torn up seat
thinking about him and all the rides we used to take in it
seeing miss ass cheeks strut past the bleachers in those short-shorts
wondering how many kids she was cooking pancakes for right now
and if her new boyfriend beat her like her first two husbands had

I reached under the seat and pulled out an empty fifth of "old somebody"
my hand brushing against something that half-rolled, half-rattled
reaching back under the seat I extracted a red plastic baseball bat
the heel of the bat had been cut nearly off and it was heavier than I remembered
pulling the flap back on the heel exposed a 35 mm film canister
…and another…and another
until finally a dozen were in my lap
the first one I opened on the kitchen table had $800 in it
mostly in 50s and 20s
by the time I had finished counting I had enough cash
to pay for my last year at vo-tech and the best set of Snap-on tools money could buy
when he came up missing we wondered if Alonzo had been carted off and done in
because of a bad drug deal or something and this confirmed it

Just for a minute I thought I smelled cigarette smoke
realizing that was his way of telling me it was okay
I said "Thanks Alonzo" out loud
walked in the front room and switched on the Cardinals
facing the Cubs at Busch stadium
popped the top on a cold beer
and waited for the man to come get the Chieftain

The Word

"What's the good word?"
Walter asked

Lip over rim
the trick of sunlight
caught the drop of coffee
as it magnetically encircled
the heel of his cup
he put it down on the table
back in the ring
it had called home
for 30 odd years
bacon frying and eggs, too
he turned to look out the window
at trucks and cars passing by
on the snow-covered highway

"Reckon it'll snow anymore?"
the fry cook replied

To no one in particular

The bacon pieces flipped
in excruciating slow motion
over the dancing griddle
the eggs offered their sunny smiles

"Why hair no!"
Walter half-grunted

The rest of us were just too damn cold to grin

Cat Shit

"I worked for one them outfits that contracts out to companies that owns them big billboards out on the freeway…musta been 12 years or so…we took the old stuff down, er what we could of it, they was layers of that stuff up there…and we put up the new ads. I lost two good friends when I worked there…they both fell about 40 feet but they was sober as a judge on a Tuesday. I never fell, at least not all the way to the ground anyhow. We used to all get us a pint on Fridays at dinner and we'd already have our buzz goin' by quittin' time. I miss that job and I miss them people"

Robert "Cat Shit" Higgins

FEMA Trailer

Forty eight hundred dollars?
gently used??
how do you know?
either of you...
the buyer
or the seller?

A baby
could have been
conceived
amid humid tension
relieved
on the weak-ass table
or the vinyl floor

It has a full size fridge
and an accordion bedroom door
three children
might have done
some homework
or scored some skunky dope
and smoked it
behind their mom's car
while she was passed out
on the jack-knife sofa
in the 70 square foot living room

A little east
of the Crescent City
off interstate 10
Roseanne episodes
blaring in the background
with little brother asleep
in the queen bed
up front

and your stoned ass
made it to a bunk
by the toilet
that never worked right

This thing looks pretty rough
on the outside
I think I'll pass

Dust

That morning I heard birds singing
but didn't pay much attention to them
I smelled good coffee coming from the kitchen
Mary had left a fresh pot brewing
we'd made love on our waking
a great start to a vacation day

I lingered in bed
while she got the kids ready
I didn't get up to kiss them bye
stressing over stress release
thinking about this vacation
our bills
how could we afford it?
I heard the faucet dripping in the bath
and the toilet that wouldn't stop running
I threw the covers back and stomped off to the shower

It was good to pull on jeans
no tie today
hard-soled shoes gave way to hikers
grabbing a cup
I headed off to run a crucial errand
an oil change for the SUV
but first run into the city
get some files from the office for the weekend
Mary frowned on work when we went to Cape Cod
I was shooting for a promotion, so I'd have to sneak them in

I parked in my normal spot three blocks away
and walked up to the North Tower
waited what seemed like an eternity
for an elevator
going up 97 floors
was never a fast ride

today it seemed to drag on in excess

As the elevator opened onto my office floor
I was met with a soul crunching wave of negative energy
accompanied by the sound of a roaring sea
set into motion by an earthquake
it was not even 9 yet

I was consumed by it shortly thereafter
I didn't feel any pain or cry out
at the moment of what must have been my mortal release
I thought I could smell coffee and hear birds
I thought about my kids and Mary
the missed exchange of "I love you" with them that morning
I thought about the dripping faucet and laughed out loud

Physically transformed into smoky dust
later settling over lower Manhattan
my ghost haunts Cape Cod
seeking refuge in the evening cool of the dunes
forever losing all track of time

Treasure On The Ground

Can't figure out why
they haven't caught me yet
maybe nobody cares what I'm doing
out here with the coyotes and owls
so damn far back Wooly Road
I don't hear the chainsaws no more

The best things about living out here
no school
and Daddy's still here

I can talk to him whenever I need to
especially when I don't know what to do
his answer may not come right away
but he always answers

Sometimes I hear his voice
in a dream or doing chores
telling me what I need to do
to make things right
that's how I fixed the pump

Right after he died
I put him in Granddad's
old Fleetwood in the barn
I'd worry that they'd find out
and I'd have to start back to school
got some big old grain truck tarps
to throw over the car
I remember the smile on his face
when I pulled them down over the windshield
and anchored it down with rocks

Thought the smell might bring them running
guess we're just so far back in here it didn't matter

it went away after about a year
That's when I first heard him talking to me

It took a while, maybe two more years
before I could look inside the Fleetwood and talk back to him
when I finally did it was like we'd never missed a day

I told him about cutting my foot real bad that first winter with the ax
how I'd kept the taxes up on the farm like he'd showed me
when he taught me how to write a check in 8th grade
just before he got sick

Tonight the smoke from the woodstove
hangs in the trees like fog
and we have a good talk

"Yeah, Daddy your government money is still comin' in. That drillin'
company keeps on sendin' money to that bank account you put in my
name."

"Nah, I'm eatin' real good. hardly never see nobody 'cept when I go
get groceries and I go all the way over to Hardin to get 'em where
people don't know me."

"Yeah, sometimes I do get lonesome. I want a woman. I looked at one
for a long time and follered her around in the Sav-A-Lot last week. She
acted so scared so I quit doing it. Nah, I'm afraid no woman would
ever understand about me and you…."

"Oh, some…I tried to squirrel hunt down in the pecan orchard last
week. The wind was blowing too bad. I do..I do remember what you
said about the wind….and the water….Some days they love you and
some days they hate you."

"When I quit huntin' that day I started lookin' for arrowheads. I don't
know what made me look at this dirt clod but there she was. This little
ole bitty thing. reckon them Indians used it for birds? Ain't a chip out

of place on it…..treasure on the ground. Ain't nobody seen it in a thousand years. Sorta like you. I'm gonna leave it with you. put it in the ashtray here where it will be safe."

"I gotta go now Daddy and stir up the fire. I'll be back to see you soon."

The Line Judge

He walks
with a heavy hand
and a wandering eye
a flask of whiskey
glued to his hip pocket
feeding rattlesnakes
on grasshoppers
keeping them
from real flesh
insects have no bones
nor motivation
for upward mobility

I am a beetle then

Significant Events

Air can be compressed
as can any gas
but in order to be compressed
it must be contained
there is no container large enough
to hold the air I breathe
high winds
swift current
sickness
have not taken me away
no pennies rest
on my eyes
many before me
many after me
live life more reckless
or more quietly
I'm in the middle of the road
after swerving
from one side
to the other

Pea Patch

In the gloaming hours
of a late summer afternoon
you could feel the cool
seep up from the ground
we'd swat mosquitoes
and fill up buckets
full of purple hull peas
the soft ground
crunched like brown sugar
under foot
there was more said to one another
in that pea patch
than was ever said
round a dinner table
it continued on
when the peas were shelled
and fingers turned purple
reminding us
of our labor
and the blood
that brought us together

Early Summer Gloaming (Long Ago)

Innocence remembered
in the season's first pair
of cut-off jeans
alternating
warm and cool breezes
on pasty legs
laughing
shadowy children
chase fireflies
serenaded
by 13-Year Cicadas
Mason jar
poorly ventilated
now a light fixture
shimmering and flashing
sunburnt faces
against the backdrop
of an Oldsmobile hubcap
mulberries
staining bare feet
on the walk home
purple
like the sky

Black Coffee

My head was propped up
on biscuits and sausage gravy
I want to smell it again
not the fancy stuff
they drink now
the real stuff
taken black
in diners and church fellowship halls
after weddings and funerals
the bottomless cup
the first time I drank it
was New Year's Eve
as a child
I begged for it
they let me have it
reluctantly
at the behest of a tipsy friend
"It won't kill him"
it tasted
like liquid black pepper
without the sting
I stayed up until 3 am

By the Minute

When I was a kid
about 12
I shot pool
for a penny a minute
at the local pool hall
on 8 foot slate tables
with leather criss-cross
drop pockets
just happened to be
the back part
of a DX service station

Two friends
usually showed up to shoot pool
after school
when *Star Trek* or
The Wild, Wild West re-runs ended

When I started out
I sucked at it
as most do
I don't know anybody
that was given the skill
as a birth gift

We played *8 Ball*
as partners
one man out, but
my favorite game was
Cut-throat

My father was a gambler
in his early days
would blow his paycheck
on Friday night

against a guy
he knew he couldn't beat
my mom would get so mad
that she'd buy a new dress
on credit when he lost

The guy my dad never beat
taught me how to "shoot for shape"
"On your next shot...after you make this one"
in the back room of a dx service station
the best lesson I ever had

"Shoot for shape"
still rings true nearly 40 years later
and I try to do that by the minute

Grit

I was intrigued by the prizes
that could be "won"
from the back pages
of the rag I peddled
for two summers
nobody bought it
because they wanted to read it

You couldn't take the colors for real
photos in aquamarine
60s leftovers
a trace of 70s
we got the news too late
haircuts were 7 years out of style
but those old women
felt sorry for me
and bought a subscription
the printed word was their outlet
for human contact

January 1973
murder, crisis, Hollywood
and cars passed by on the highway
just feet away from our house
of confinement and malcontent

Lately

He asks...
"How are things at work?"
lately he says
"How are the wife and kids?"
lately he says
"I just don't know about Ford...
do you think they'll go under??"
lately he thinks
..."I don't want to die alone"
lately they think
"What will I do if the other one dies first?"
"Go to the Bahamas"...they think
lately he says
"I wonder if you love me."
I say "Yeah, dad...I do"
lately he says
"I know you raised yourself"
lately he says
"I missed doing things with you"
lately he says
"You can thank your mother for pushing you on"
lately he says
"You know I love you, don't you?"
lately I think
"Yeah... I do"

My Father's House

His house has a characteristic smell
I used to think it was cigarette smoke
from years of two people smoking
two packs a day each inside its paneled walls
I remember the fog hanging when I was a kid
like I imagined a bar would be
while they cussed each other and fought
after we'd been to church
turns out I was right about the bars
but the house hasn't been smoked in
for 20 years

I thought for a while
it might just be a musty smell
from so many years
of closed windows
mom thought the roaches could get in
under the screens
I imagined them leaving the neighbors' houses
bindles tied to a stick
headed for the land of milk and honey
like so many Dust Bowl refugees
just like them, the roaches would be in for a surprise
once they reached their destination
I think the reason pests never took up residence
was because they couldn't be comfortable there

I never felt safe there
you never knew when hell was coming down
or you'd get it for rubbing your finger
down the side of a dusty car

It all came to a head after 51 years
Mom took her last punch one summer
and he was left there alone

She got the blood money
He got the brick and mortar

The house stands empty as I write this
awaiting a new owner
while the ghosts of turmoil haunt the narrow gaps
in the corners of the baseboards
warning unknowing spiders of their impending demise

On the way home from work today
I ran over a snake and shivered
just for a minute I smelled his house
and realized
what I had been smelling
all those years
was fear

I love them both

Flagging Down The Devil

I was sick
in the backseat
reading an Archie comic
the Impala
was rolling up
"scenic"
Highway 7
My father at the wheel
My mother was the navigator
destination: Dogpatch, USA

It was like a low-rent
Silver Dollar City
if you can imagine that
I could almost smell
the trout swimming
in Mill Creek in anticipation
I really needed to puke
but choked it back

Just then my mother shrieked
"There's a woman in the ditch!"
My father kept going
a quarter mile past
curiosity or guilt
made him 180
and there she was

Her face was painted
with lipstick
and who knows what

A great big bearded guy
in overalls showed up
driving an International Harvester pickup

the stopping of the heap
sounded like the train stop
on *Petticoat Junction*

The bearded one offered
"She does this all the time"
without emotion
he helped her into the IH
we traveled on to Dogpatch

Instamatic pics
of the rest of that trip
were made into slides
but nothing sticks in my mind
more than the woman in the ditch
the lipstick
and the smell of dead trout
that shouldn't have been there
in the first goddamn place

Changing Hands

My farm had a fence
the fence had two gates
one used often
the other seldom
a latch held closed the most-used gate
a chain the other
the latch was oiled and maintained
the chain was left to the elements
exposed to hot and cold
wind, sun, rain, sleet, and snow
the chain grew rusty
the gate blew open
a broken link was the cause
a bright new chain replaced it
unprotected, it assumed this new role
unaware of the fate that lies ahead
envious of the latch
that is never replaced

Maple

He stood among them
his own people
mother and father
aunts, uncles, cousins
old friends of the family
his family
yet on that hot July day
he felt oddly and
unremarkably alone
the White River Boys
-he was one-
let her casket down
low in the red moist earth
her ghost sat above
on the green funeral tent
bobbing in the soft breeze
shuffling a thick deck of cards
happy that all were there
but equally aware of that boy's isolation

African Violets

She had a toaster oven
I think I tested the warranty
baking sweetness
in the form of butter and sugar toast
washed down with a glass of tang
the astronauts on Skylab drank it you know

"Honey, I don't care for what you eat.
I'm just afraid it will make you sick
if you eat too much", she'd say

Not really looking at me
just being careful not to spill
the W.E. Garrett glassful of water
nourishment meant for the African Violets
in little clay flower pots
soaking up love in the window

Shield

"Come in this house!"
heat bouncing off
the warm morning stove
soaking into chilled bones
like the snow
from the walk over
had drowned
navy blue Chuck Taylors

Her house was always
a good place to hide
and lick wounds
when the shit got thick
and made me feel older
than 10 or 12
"Tired through the eyes"
she called it

Her lemon icebox pie
could sway Anton Lavey
and it seemed like
powdered drink mixes
replenished themselves
in her pantry
overnight
without effort
killer sweets
just showed up
like miracles
but she was a Baptist

I could've stayed
as long as I'd wanted
if it'd been up to her
but eventually

I'd have to go back

Later on I learned
she'd done the same
for older cousins
who'd had it much worse

I hope I never have to be her

Old Testament

"Are there such things as ghosts?"
the little boy asked

"The dead know nothing" she said
and put away the groceries

Bread, hot dogs, sugar, and tang
the cool air trickled in through the rusty screens
I wondered what she meant
her response offered up
to a skinny little boy's question about ghosts
the dead are not real
they don't see, talk, or feel
afternoons of Ecclesiastes
Match Game '70-something
Bluto and Sweet Pea
Olive Oyl and Cap'n Crunch
Beanie and Cecil and Hercules
with a guided muscle

Today this middle-aged, mis-guided man
still wonders about her response

Tomato

I thought I smelled you today

Camels and body odor
burned my nose
about 1:30 pm
out in the garden
picking Better Boys

It just had to be you

I looked up
from my labor
thinking you'd be there
disappointed that you weren't

Basketball Seasons

We spent many hours
turning clay into dust
in the summer
wonder how many dribbles
it took to do that?

If you left the ball
out in the cold
it would go almost flat
somedays it was hell
to find a needle
on snow days
our coach
would open the gym
if we could find him
otherwise
a Monopoly marathon ensued

A teammate spit
on the bleachers once
while getting our asses chewed
after losing a game we shoulda won
the coach said

"That's disgusting! Don't spit in here!"

Then he lifted the cigarette to his lips
and took a hard pull

Sand

There was a place I hung out at
when I was about 13 years old
a Freewill Missionary Baptist church
where I would be baptized and married
a few short years later

The church had some construction going on then
a fellowship hall addition was being built
that whole summer
a vacant concrete slab was there
for the taking

I was a no-shit skater
polyurethane wheels and plastic decks
ruled back then
but I had a fiberglass deck
with a kick ass kick tail

I remember conversations
about *Fleetwood Mac* and *Eddie Money*
a horrible waste of my young breath
I remember the wheels of that skateboard
grinding on sand when you least expected it
sometimes it would stop you in your tracks
other times just piss you off and you'd keep going

Since those days have passed
I've been to several weddings and funerals
in that fellowship hall
as soon as I set foot in the building
I think about the sand
that probably still remains
under the indoor/outdoor carpet
and how it tried to stop me
from flying

Waiting on 15

We sat there and waited
until half-way through
the third quarter
I was nervous as hell
she had her hand
in my front pocket
leg pressed close to my hip

She was the first to suggest
that we both meet outside
at the start of the fourth quarter
I had an orange 9 volt transistor radio
turned it on when we got to the bus
Poco and WLS coming in
as we were kissing
my tongue taking the bubble gum taste
to the back of her throat
I saw a deacon of my church
walk by in the corner of my eye
and he gave me the "thumbs up"

I spelled "team"
with an "I" that night

That Old Black Dog

I grew up in a circus of sorts
to say the least
an only child
I was the referee
by default, of my parents' near daily skirmishes
in a war that still goes on to this day

From about 12 years old
my friends and I
cut from common cloth
hung out together
escaping into the night
trying to stay out of trouble
but usually not trying hard enough
most times
we'd have so much fun that we'd forget
about what was going on back home
just glad to be missing it

In those days
the outskirts of the town I grew up in
had become a dumping ground
for unwanted dogs
I think the pack
that slept under an overgrown hedge
just up the road from my house
must have known instinctively
that a mother would feed them scraps at a back door
but fathers might not be so kind

One of my favorite poets wrote
"Angels and dogs are not very different at 2:30 in the afternoon"
maybe he was right

I cruised around town on Frankenstein's monster

a BMX bicycle of sorts scabbed together
from scavenged carcasses
their missing parts long gathering ghosts
it squeaked and whined and limped along
as if the rims were square
and the tin man had lost his oil can
this monstrosity that carried me homeward
following evenings of merriment with my wayward pals
would sometimes awaken the pack of dogs
as they slept under the hedge
and they'd give chase

The pack had an unspoken leader
in an un-bobbed Doberman mix
we'd dubbed *Virgil the Spider Dog*
he earned this moniker due to the long tail
and legs that seemed to uncoil when he stood up
showing him to be at least a head taller
than the four-legged foot soldiers of his army
my own sneaker clad foot had been nipped by Virgil
on more than one occasion
and I was scared to death of him
trouble was, I rarely, if ever thought about him
until he was already in fast pursuit
flashing his teeth and growling low
leaving me to think
I should have done what I'd thought about
for a split second three hours earlier
and pedaled the long way home
in order to avoid their lair

Even as much as it made me uncomfortable to be there
there was something about my yard
that made the mongrels give up chase
and fade away like a vapor trail from a high flying jet
some invisible boundary stood
and they would not venture to cross it

so if I could just make it
to the yard, then up on the carport
without getting bitten
it would all be okay
the duality of it ironic
I had tried so hard to escape it before darkness fell
I tried even harder, it seemed, to get back to it

Figuratively, at 48 years of age
the black dog still chases me
and it chases us all
I realized only a few short months ago
the trick to avoid getting bitten
is to simply stop pedaling and coast
this confuses what we most fear
and I've lived through some of my darkest
I'm still squeaking and limping along on square wheels
slower, yes, but I always seem to make it to the carport

Cornbread

We all heard the pistol shot
sounded like a firecracker
they'd been at it for hours
whiskey finally won out
the Po-po showed
just a flesh wound....
but next weekend
me and my cousin
were skateboarding
interrupted by shouting
peered around
the stone corner
of the Methodist church
and watched two guys
go at it
with a 2 x 4
and a log chain

The guy with the 2 x 4 lost the fight

Years later…..
the "loser" was a county Po-po himself
I was underage
with Miller Highlife pony beers
in an arcade parking lot
talking to 15 year old girls
of wealthy statesmen

"If you will pour all your beer out
right here, leave and not come back tonight
I'll let you go"

We poured out
the remaining 3
of the original 48 beers

went back home
got in another vehicle
came back to town
and laughed at the world

Seasonal Witch

I saw tobacco
fly from the end
of her custom-roll cigarettes
in the early spring
and early fall
sparks searching
for the fires of hell
or a balcony seat
for the matinee in heaven
she raised six boys
that I know of

She knew the change
of the season
like a fox
she was rough as a cob
ugly in the face
beautiful in the soul
faded green lines
on forearms
told the story
...almost

Under a cloud of smoke
near as tall as her
I heard her say once...

*"Hell boys, if the world didn't spin
we'd all have a turd in our hip pocket"*

Her family stole her body
had a party with her
danced with her
broke her legs
shared their beer and cigarettes with her

They went to jail
but she went down happy

Disturbed

Thursday…

She had all she could stand
left after her shift
at the button factory
went by the house and
picked up her brother's .410
drove to the north side
of the old ferry
blew the left side of her head off
over some worthless piece of shit

Saturday…

My basketball coach
came into my grandma's cafe
asked nervously to use the phone
to call the sheriff

"I got a dead woman on my trot line"

We all went down to take a look
I had nightmares about her
coming out behind my dad's recliner
I wasn't sure if she wanted to talk
or wanted to take me with her
to another dark place

Not Lost

I can't remember her name
but like all good southern girls
she had two of them
the second one
might have been Michelle
or Ann
we just spent a few hours together
my mother introduced us
the daughter of a friend

I was probably four or five
she a bit older
it was spring
there was a tire swing
she had leukemia
I didn't know what it was
mother was worried
she'd get hurt while we played
she didn't seem to enjoy life
as much as I did

At that age
most people
don't know much
about anything
but I could tell she was tired
I'm pretty certain she died
shortly after we met

Funny how forty years go by
and a faded memory
can reach out

Maybe she was here today

Before the Harvest

A rice field in august
in the White River bottoms
smells like a clean fish
you have to smell it for yourself
to understand what that means
but once you do
it will never leave your brain

I remember hot nights
and mosquitoes
a blue jean girl
with kisses so soft
and breasts so firm
you didn't care
if you woke up
much less where

There was always shame
that worthless emotion
tugging on the ropes
of the auditorium curtain
exposing the slightest weakness

Even unpopular people
needed to get laid

I remember names
and test scores
from that time
and I wonder
if that bitch
is still working
at the bank□

American Youth

Lonely women asked us questions
about hot dates and making out
their noses and asses
wiped on the same cloth
in turn they accused us
we were the usual suspects
rounded up
when rocks were thrown
tombstones pushed over
old ferry boats cut loose
piss-drunk hitch-hiking neighbors
given 10 mile rides to their doorstep
darkness never took us
it just borrowed us
sometimes a minute, sometimes years
a constant battle between doing right
at least what they considered was right
and what might have made us
who we were meant to be
most of us just gave in
my advice to the youth of America
always wonder
what you will be remembered for
it will make you live longer
don't wake up at 50
and tell yourself
"I could have been good at that"
don't run away from responsibility
don't create if you can't handle it
and when the darkness comes in
keep one foot in the light
I'll leave it up to you
to close the door

Waiting

I was waiting for you
in 1982
on a bleak, cold
morning in March
to tell me
you didn't
love me anymore

I'm still waiting

You never did

That makes me happy
30 years later

All these other
unlucky motherfuckers
never rode
the rollercoaster
never bit the leather
never had to worry about more
than what number
they'd eat off the Mexican menu
they had their lives
laid out ahead of them
when they were still kicking
in the womb

I'm still trying
to find mine

About A Train

When I first read
Joe Klein's fine book

Woody Guthrie: A Life

I was in grad school
carrying a full semester
working two part-time jobs
second baby on the way

There were some pretty stressful moments
to say the least

During that time
I made a poor attempt to be many things
father, husband, student, teacher, and worker

Not enough salt in the shaker

As I read about Woody
I admired this little man
that seemed to have the courage
of a thousand armies
he'd pick up and hop a box car
to points unknown at the drop of a hat
leaving his life and family behind

One afternoon leaving work
I saw a slow moving train
headed east out of town
the open box cars rattled by
I could hear the sirens call

"Hop on old boy. I'll take you for a ride."

I thought about what life could be
if I just hopped on
let the train drive me
thought how easy it would be
to run alongside
pull myself up
just like Woody did
time and time again

Of course I didn't do it
I watched the thing
warble and wobble its way
to a "leaving town speed"
and went home to my family

25 years have passed by
I read more about Woody
listened more to his music
met Alan Lomax in Memphis in the 90s
talked about Woody to other admirers
celebrated his legend in Okemah
I'm still a huge fan of his story and life's work

But as I sit here tonight
by this fire in January
my wife and grandson close by

I have to wonder

Which one of us
was really more courageous
about a train?

Light Floods In

There it is
shining

Revealing
God
as the third baseman
I wanted to be as a kid
as the hobo
we gave a back porch meal to
as the talk show host
we watched late at night
when the world was asleep

Deliver us
from each other
but let me see
your face
one more time
clouded by dust
particles
dancing
in that living room sun

Asleep

Last night
I watched you
as you slept
and I saw a theatre
of life
sprawl out
on your face

Unaware
that my mind
or pen
recorded
your history

Yet it was all there

Maternal grandfather
I see his chin

Vague lines of worry
earned
by honest measure

Mother to more
than you bore
but mother, yes
just the same

Beauty and honor even at rest

I wish for you
peace and calmness
a lifetime of rest
the kind you had last night
One Word

With one word
she can tear down the barricades
the warriors of my soul have constructed
with the next
they are heaved erect to stand again
she knows the letters and syllables
are there on the other side
they lie there awaiting a chance
to escape through pulses
through motion
through sight
through ink
into paper
but not into this room

Love Walks In

Seeking refuge in a lonesome mind
love walks in an open door
a feather drifting
seeking release
from a Mexican honeymoon breeze
salt, sand and sex
July Sunday Margaritas
satiny interludes
dripped on the canvas
of carefree afternoons
love slipped out
found its escape
forgotten window unsecured
wounding memories return

Women Explode

A child asked "why?"
to his mother
naturally inquisitive
not in a smart-ass way
as the mother accused
she further responded
with the back of her hand
and sent the squealing brat packing
amidst a river of tears and haze of snot
mom lit another cigarette
and blew smoke against the window

At breakfast one morning
the couple argued over wallpaper
spoons and orange juice went sailing
as her foot pushed the little table
in his general direction
a glass tumbler shattered on the tile floor
she never apologized for the cut above his eye
but worried about the blood stain on the rug

An encounter
in late July
back in *The Day*
standing up against a car
outside her house
she rode me
like a horse
and bit my neck
right at "The Moment"
I thought I heard her whimper

Only Human

Drawn to them
true beauty
flowing tresses
smell of lavender
fragile cross on a gold chain
explores the crevice
mixing metaphor
of saintly sin
every curve
fuels the fire
leads to thoughts
of what lies beneath

If You Get Me

If you get me
you get the warts
the ugly parts
the sunny side up

If you get me
you get spring weeds
mints and dandelions
watercress and cabbage

If you get me
you go to jail with me
weddings too
we know all the family secrets
buried parents
grandparents alike

If you get me
I get you
we're both spinning
grasping
at the world
as it spins
on a broken axis
of time
not fade away

Daughter

Do you remember
counting stars
before the sun went down?
the trampoline
was a hammock
we could feel
October
seeping underneath
bare legs and feet

"Daddy it's cold"

You were two
I was barely 30
we went inside
at dark
watched a cowboy movie
with mom and brother
you fell asleep
under my arm

Today I saw
a young woman
walk out of
my house
and into
a cruel old world

Jumping Off

Waves wash up
driftwood, shells, dead things
salty air under leaden clouds
forces humans indoors
gulf coast deluge
not uncommon

Mid-morning libations
shift thoughts to wander
opening neurological files
45 year old hard drive
the design eludes Microsoft
to this day

Remembering a house
remodeled on Charles Street
26 years before
three-quarter inch hole
kitchen bare plywood floor
shoddily patched
flimsy filler
hidden by bright linoleum
was it ever discovered?

Compared to this
I am nothing more

A fake, an outlander, infidel flying under the radar
of so-called contemporary peers
pretending to take notes
showing interest in writings
they no doubt must read
while engaging in late-night self-abuse
or otherwise verbal coitus

I am not them

Tall oaks hold on
to lazy green rustling leaves
how many cells make up your being?
how much heart is in a soul?
how many thoughts remembered?
how many chosen to forget?

Payment

The backdrop
of my daily commute
is peppered with all manner
of advertising media
for the businesses along the corridor
mostly for the purchase
of protection or nourishment
of some sort

Abundant Life Ministries

Shelter Insurance

Ace Liquor Center

Cici's Pizza

It made me think this morning
that we really just rent these life necessities
comfort, joy, sustenance
then I turned up Son Volt
on satellite radio
got what I needed for the day
brought to me
by the best damn $22.43 I spent this month

Shake Out Yo Rug

Ants and people
are not so much different
species guided by a leader

Rumpled edges
must be unfolded
smoothed into calm
like bricks
set up on a course

Sometimes
a person
has to stay awake
for 36 hours
to run all the bits and pieces
out of their head
like emptying out
an ice tray
in front of God and everybody
watching their most intimate thoughts
and actions be judged
as they collect
in the gutter

They Left

Fifty years ago
white folks
got the hell outta
Little Rock
because a TV anchorman's son
got his ass beat at school
probably due
to assholish behavior
less to do
than being white

They left
by the droves
just the same
scared running
left grandpa's spiders
in the window casing
left the air tank
behind the door
of the garage
full of air
no direction
upon escape

Today they are returning
fighting to get
a reasonable mortgage
they'll live by anybody
no shame

Holidays more pleasant
than any known before

Tell again why they left to begin with?

Wire

It holds the broken pieces
of glass together
if someone or something
penetrates the surface of the window
they line up like cattle
when the truck carrying hay
comes to the gate
for the chance to smoke
waiting and drinking coffee by the pint
dinner break at 4:30 pm
I hate Jewel
We all hate the way
this chick here sings her songs
we ask for the short version
of each selection
but I can't blame anybody for this
I did this to me

Profit Margin

When the mercury is high
and the humidity is higher
I like to come in early
on a weekday afternoon
to crawl inside a beer bottle
hide out in this cool, dark place
from anything and everything
just sit and drink

Sometimes I'll feed the jukebox
it has real records that skip once in a while
none of that mp3 shit
the bartenders all know me
they keep the beer coming
my mind begins to roll on things like

How many gallons of beer do the taps draw in a week?
How many asses have graced the frayed vinyl barstools?

How many have hooked up in here late on a Saturday night?

Maybe the deed was done in a restroom stall
while a loud band and laughter
covered the sounds of drunken casual love
how much rent money
has been lost at the pool table
or drank up on this very stool where I sit
while kids went without milk at home?

How many spouses or significant others
have come in here searching for someone
and pulled them away at closing time?
It seems everybody pays
not just the patrons

While I sit here in this cold, empty tomb
the weekend regulars are at work
sweating to make toasters or flush radiators
whatever it is they do
to make the money that pays their tab
when the heart beats to life
Friday at 5
pumping out buck-fifty PBRs
and three dollar well drinks

God. I love this place.

Dream in 4/4 Time

You stood by him
not in a loud bar this time
in your mother's front yard
after the movie
you'd stopped to pick up your daughter
chill of November
made you press your lithe body
against his
you kissed
at that moment he realized
what you had meant about sharks
the first time you'd met
He realized he'd been one

Relentless
hopeless
full of risk and guilt

Even though he'd been forgiven
by the words you'd typed
not by the words of your heart

Burning Boxes

A leftover robin
chirps a weak phrase
over Hank Williams
protecting the nest
from the human eye
that strains to see
what the wild world
sees clearly
labitae before sassafras

I'm burning things
in the backyard
thinking
how fire cleanses
awash
and provides
a new beginning
taking mental notes
a beer box
becomes *The Scream*
flame applied
at just the exact measure

Autumn floats in
on a distant Dollar Store rug
freedom close behind

Bird Shit

Hottest day of the year
crack an egg
hold it in cupped hands
see what happens
he sat on his back porch
imbibing
cool libation
no worries
loose neck

Friendly neighbor
waves as he enters the pool
he waves back
takes another sip
neighbor begins the ritual
weekly vacuum
scrubbing
chemicals
he watches neighbor sweat
in water for at least an hour
water sparkling
rays of death deceiving
while the devil disguised
as a mourning dove
swoops down from above
releasing uric acid from the gut
into the pristine H_2O

Blood drains from face of neighbor

He takes another sip
chuckling almost knowingly
such is life

Those Boys

Ran the streets
ran from everything
only let time catch up
if they couldn't ride the horse
they were scared
didn't want anyone to know it
when they slowed down
really slowed down
to let life in
they figured out was okay to be scared
everybody is always learning
always growing
watching everybody else
do the same

Garrison

It
has always
been with us
lurking
breeding
making itself
stronger
snickering
at failed attempts
of aversion
a temporary diversion
was the best
that we could do

Christians
might say
It
is the Devil
It
has a name

Garrison

She did back-flips
between the crepe myrtles
when bad things happened
She was the maestro
of orchestrated chaos

The Horse
rode up
in little baggies
burned our spoons
and found its way
into veins

leaving blood
on the ceiling
and death
in the cracks
between
the floorboards

We hoped *Garrison*
had latched on
to a bum's ball sac
and caught a bus
to New Orleans
not as much as
a giggle
from the garden
for two months

Then I let the dog out
to pee tonight
and heard
that old familiar
snort

By A Thread

I still can't believe
I did it
You goaded me into it
I'd been perfectly happy
to watch the super scary movie

Frankenstein

Dracula

The Creature from God Knows Where

You called me a *pussy*
that was as good
as a triple dog dare

You did it
to watch me fall down
and act stupid
providing entertainment
for all the creatures of the night
taking my innocence
feeding your need to destruct
the first ride was free

You created a paying customer
steal…lie…rob…
maybe even kill
to ride it again

This morning I heard
what I thought was a child's voice
turn out to be a ringtone from 2003
that fuzzy memory
must have summoned you back

from the edge of the woods
and into the field
beside the pump house
I stared you down
from the trailer steps
shaking my head
yelling "GIT!!"

I watched you vaporize
felt the burning in my arm subside
strengthened for now
but hanging on
by a thread

Nobody Sleeps

5 am
an hour before waking
all these houses
start to stir
ceremonial brewing
of coffee beans
Folger's or Seattle's Best
nectar of encouragement
or simply lubrication
for conversation

Eventually
someone
or a tribe
applies
metal to acid
and petrol to a flame
to engage
with humanity
another work day
money changes hands
shares are traded
the sun sets
burgers are consumed
steaks and drinks too
deals are sealed

While people
that did this
30 years ago
lay dying in nursing homes

Trace

The river of blood
feeds a well of forever

Anna is *different*
so we must be
especially nice to her
we must help her
transcend ...
she's smart
smarter than you
smarter than me

The ladies
from the Baptist church
will come see her
and her family
bringing fudge
and cookies
taking gossip
leaving chaos
in their wake

Husbands
will have to make
excuses
mistresses
won't talk

They all die eventually

Something We Work For

Might be there

Might not

You'd think
there has to be
a secure footing
on the ladder
at some elevation
that provides
a semi-comfortable
path towards grasping
the chalice

Fading away
all these hours
spent falsifying
an existence

It might pay off

some day

but when?

God's Table

When I drive through here
I see that God
has set a table
for a Sunday dinner
I probably don't see the table
as those who live here would see it

Tan brick houses with carports
crippled school buses in pastures
that last felt the footsteps of children
when Joe Namath played football

The kids that rode the bus are adults now
hoping for a decent retirement
and social security to be there
in 25 years

God has set a table for them
but he doesn't care whether they eat or not
he just wants them to clean up

The Pinta

She was red and Japanese
never refused to comply
though not much out of the ordinary
was asked of her
she provided shelter
from the elements
to a weary drunk
never left him stranded
always brought him safely back home
from trips to Rehab Mountain
Ohio, Alabama, Okemah
Memphis and Nashville
with a little bit of Motown in her soul
She rides the ribbon still
taking someone else
to places they think they have to be

Trees Don't Complain

Trees don't complain
when the weight of their fruit
snaps their branches
prior to a bountiful harvest

Trees don't complain
when straight-line winds
bend and twist them
in a late April thunderstorm

Trees don't complain
as they are cut down
processed into floors and firewood
or give up their life for the printed word

Trees don't complain
they provide shade
for this house
while the truth is side-stepped

Cardinal

What is that crimson
that flutters in the snow?
nearer in image
to bloody paper
glued to a puppet
Cardinal, dead not long
non-migratory
against winter's fury
turning to strangers
cracking handout seeds
in a powerful beak

Can sustain
for a time

The sharp whistle begs
old men and women
interrupted from morning coffee
they cannot resist the call
to provide the daily allotment

An English Sparrow
brown and gruff
seeks shelter
between my house
and that of my dog
doesn't take advantage

Merely waits for the snow to melt

A Crow's Breakfast

The Low Road is devoid
of warm carrion
in early misty light
Mayhans for breakfast it will be
the old bird is wise
knowing to stay away
when humans are in the orchard
knows what they are thinking
human things
mostly surrounded by worry

Extracting lunch
from the bark of a dead elm
electric black and feathered
they'd welcome a spyglass
to find them

Some have drinking glass wings
veined and bigger than their bodies
feeding too on what once lived
offering little nutritional value
hollow like the bones of their predator

Evening roost brings rest
to synapse
strengthens instinct
preparing for another day

Prometheus Returns

I saw a trail of gray smoke
leave the chimney
of the house on the hill
tried to trace it back in my mind's eye
past a lip of mortar
flowing backward
across soot-darkened bricks
more mortar pushed out around their edges

When the chimney was first fired
chunks of the stuff fell into the fire.....

Tracing into a gap of invisible pungent gases
before re-entering the orange flame
and leaping into a sliver of hickory
into a mixture of water and air
pulled from a stack just outside the door
placed neatly in the dry under-roof on the porch
cleaved from a log cut from a felled tree
alive on the wind
up from a seed
meeting fertile soil

Dating Sinead O'Connor

The Bible says
it is wrong to lie
about anything
so here it is

Okay...

We never really "dated"
as much as compared notes
on being abused as children
we blueprinted our shoplifting techniques
that we'd honed to perfection
way before Winona got busted
and made it all the shit
these subjects discussed
over warm beer
stolen pot
smoked oysters
and dry cigarettes

Lying on the warm hood of a parked car
she would sing like a siren even back then

Evergreen…..Summertime….A Day in The Life

She liked dice and dominos
and chanting
her mother hated her
or was jealous maybe
and the feelings
were mutual I'm sure

The last time I saw her in person
was at her mother's wake
crying like she did later all over MTV

Folksinger

Way back in 1975
rock and roll was dead
and disco was alive
Bob Dylan
got his third wind
started singing for real
it was *deja vu*
all over again
he put on some makeup
tried to be somebody else
if only for a moment
he could escape himself
on stage
amidst rolling thunder
in a driving rain
neither Ramblin' Jack Elliott
nor Roger McGuinn
could make Robert Zimmerman
a folksinger again
so he found Jesus

Love Songs

The older I get
the more I realize
those songs I listened to
in my youth
were written by young men
not the elders I thought them to be

Songs about Devils in blue dresses
songs about wanting something or somebody so much
you'd kill for it

We became what we wanted
through song
made love to what we wanted
through song

Old men still dream
hoping the Devil
still finds them attractive
and worth that apple
offered and accepted
in the beginning
hoping that there will be
a riverside acre
in the promised land

We're just too tired to write about it

Thumbing Stations

I drive to work
thumbing stations
on a satellite radio
as big
as a ruled
3 x 5 note card
settling on music
pulled from a place
way back in my mind
sitting on a dusty carpet
in my grandmother's house
those words came through
a brown Bakelite radio

Harry Chapin
nobody could write the story song better

She took off to find the footlights/ I took off to find the sky

For a minute I was 8 years old
feeling safe and content

Brother Jack

Soybeans were nearly unheard of then
cotton was king of the Delta
seemed like everybody was poor

He was working on a Saturday
little brother gone fishing
made a mistake with the saw
it was unforgiving
He lost his best friend
flesh and blood
is flesh and blood after it all

JR was haunted by him   ˋ
all those years, even into old age
that tragic cut and then

Emptiness

He chased it away
with booze and pills
read the gospel for dessert

As I write this
I realize I am not far off
the walking contradiction
myself

Meanwhile the wind
is blowing softly
from the west
in Dyess Colony today
moving a little more
of Mississippi County
toward that big river

Mansfield

I saw that name
on the back of a urinal
in a public house
splattered with piss

Mansfield

My mind went quickly
struck like lightning
to black and white photos
crisp, pleated low-slung dresses
caging tits
as big as Pennsylvania

Box office success spoiled her
and Rock Hunter both
not many know
she made a movie
with Jimi Hendrix
"As Clouds Drift By"

Three times married
She spoke five languages
claimed her IQ to be 163
She was a protestant convert
to Catholicism
dabbled in Judaism
met Anton Lavey in 1966

Louisiana car crash
rumored that she lost her head
just a bad shot to the cranium

Horrible husband
and a heart-shaped headstone

kids and dogs and parakeets
pushing the flaming boat
into the mystic

Music Made Him Do It

Driving my daughter to school one morning
several years ago
we met a small green car on Arkansas 321
the young driver
looked more like he was making love
to the underside of the steering column
than driving the car
the rhythm of his movements obviously driven
by a primal thump likely produced
with high tech, state of the art recording equipment
I thought he should be focused on the road
the sunlight, the traffic, the icy patches on the asphalt

Moments later
Danny Barnes plucked a particularly
bluesy, resonant banjo lick through my car stereo speakers
it made the hairs on my neck stand up
almost chilling my spine
in my mind
I could see the strings
vibrating above the plectrum of the banjo
and realized where my attention should be focused

Voice

That voice
that ring
not the words
but they're there, too

Time spent changing
from *G* to *C*
learning St. James Infirmary
becomes a first lesson
in a minor key

Every voice
is the same

Listen
and you'll hear it too

Guitar Dreams

Last night I dreamed
I could play guitar
much better
than I have progressed
in 25+ years of fumbling
an intermediate at best
but last night....
I had a navy blue Strat
Man, I was a power chord machine
played lead like Hendrix
every note crisp
or perfectly bent
the amp was clean
no distortion
when I awoke
I picked up
that 40 year old flat top
bought with $100 and some trade
many years ago
flat-picked
a Luther Perkins lead
in the first position
over worn down frets and rosewood
and it sounded better
than I did last night
the dream interpreters
say playing a guitar in a dream
depicts harmony
hold on tight
to your dreams

The Ride

We stood in line to wait for the ticket
that slip of paper that says you have a right
we stood in line again for those tickets to be taken
we were then seated and the machine started to move
not fast as others were climbing on
we waited anxiously for the machine to speed up
finally it did and we realized that we wanted off
but it was too late
The Ride had begun

We were scared for a while
then we felt sick
all of a sudden things were calm
we were actually enjoying ourselves
then everything slowed down to a crawl
we watched the others leave the ride
one by one, two by two
until it was our turn to get off

The Ride ended quicker than it had begun
as we walked down the midway
we saw others standing in lines
some fully aware of what would happen
as they climbed aboard
others were trying out the rides
for the first time, and didn't have a clue
yet everyone would climb on
and everyone would get off

Made in the USA
Charleston, SC
09 November 2014